Faith Ride to Victory

Healing Devotional & Journal

"Don't be afraid to step out and take the faith ride to victory!"

By: Pastor Tangela Morris

Copyright © 2017 by Tangela Morris

Self-Published

All rights reserved, Printed in the United States of America. No part of this book may be reproduced in any manner whatsoever without written permission except in the case of brief quotations embodied in critical articles and reviews.

Cover Design: Modest Media Inc.
Print: CreateSpace.com
Text Set in 10-point Century School Book
Website: www.tangelamorris.com
ISBN: 978-1544145365

We can heal from several sources. The Word of God heals us, stories from others heal us, and prayer heal us.

Faith Ride to Victory!

From The Author:
Greetings!

While being victimized is not a choice, victory is. Faith Ride to Victory is a healing devotional. The writings are true writings from ladies who are either in the process of overcoming or have overcame. The words of these ladies speak not only to themselves but also to those reading this and can receive support from them.

Scripture and prayer are added by the author so that the reader can share with others and pray his/her way through the victory process. Often, we can learn and grow by connecting with others who have gone through what we are going through. This devotional is to remind you that you are not alone.

Don't be afraid to step out and enjoy the faith ride to victory ~ Pastor Tangela J. Morris

7 No More Victime. I Want the Victory!

9 *No More Victime. I Want the Victory!*

11 *No More Victim. I Want the Victory!*

13 *No More Victime. I Want the Victory!*

15 *No More Victime. I Want the Victory!*

So do not fear, for I am with you, do not be dismayed, for I am your God. I will strengthen you and help you; I will uphold you with my righteous right hand. ~ Isaiah 41:10

Dear Self,

You will become a strong amazing woman. You will have 2 wonderful children. Treasure each moment you have with them, they grow up so fast. You have a rocky road ahead of you. Just stay strong and be the best you, you can be. You will not always make the right decisions, but make your own decisions. Don't let anyone make decisions for you. When the road becomes smooth again, you will come out a better person. Always be you. ~ER

Prayer: Lord, make me whole, make me strong, and let me grow. Lord help me to make sound decisions, and know that you are always with me.

17 *No More Victime. I Want the Victory!*

18   *Faith Ride to Victory!*

19 *No More Victime. I Want the Victory!*

21 *No More Victim. I Want the Victory!*

23 *No More Victim. I Want the Victory!*

25 *No More Victime. I Want the Victory!*

27 No More Victime. I Want the Victory!

29 *No More Victime. I Want the Victory!*

Come to me, all you who are weary and burdened, and I will give you rest ~ Matthew 11:28

The road you will choose to follow will not be easy. You will do some things you are not proud of. You will hurt those you love. Every choice you make will bring you to the woman you will be. You will have a beautiful little girl. At some point, you will be broken, you will get treatment. What you will go through will make you stronger. It is not the past you can change so look forward to your future. Just know that God is always with you. ~ JS

Prayer: Lord, thank you for always being there for me and being with me. Thank you for bearing my burdens when I thought the load was too tough. Thank you for making me into the woman you desire for me to be.

33 *No More Victime. I Want the Victory!*

35 *No More Victime. I Want the Victory!*

37 *No More Victime. I Want the Victory!*

39 *No More Victime. I Want the Victory!*

41 *No More Victime. I Want the Victory!*

43 *No More Victime. I Want the Victory!*

And my God will meet all your needs according to the riches of His glory in Christ Jesus. ~ Philippians 4:19

Slow down, don't rush through life. Take your time and be a kid as long as you can. Stay in school, wait to have 5 wonderful kids. Love on your "maw maw" as much as you can. Never take a day for granted. Know that the things you will face are meant for you to help save and inspire someone else. Trust God in all things. Don't give up, your life is so important and worth it. Know your brokenness is what will make you. ~AC

Prayer: Lord, thank you for supplying all of my needs. I totally trust in you because you created me and I know that you will deliver me, save me, and guide me. Thank you for your son Jesus Christ and all that you have given me through Him.

My son (daughter) pay attention to what I say; turn your ear to my words. Do not let them out of your sight, keep them within your heart; for they are life to those who find them and health to the one's whole body. ~ Proverbs 4:20-22

You are going to face some of your hardest times. Don't rebel. Everything that is being told to you is from a place of love. You are going to turn to drugs and at first, they will be your closest friend but will end up bringing bitterness, hurt and pain. Before you lose everything, run to your family! Embrace their love and authority. You have a kind, caring, and soft heart. It's what makes you beautiful. Don't rob yourself of that. This is life or death. Choose LIFE. ~AC

Prayer: Lord, thank you for letting me choose LIFE. For I could have not done it without you, each and every day that I breathe help me to recognize your miracles and your blessings. Thank you for your Word that covers and keeps me.

49 *No More Victime. I Want the Victory!*

51 *No More Victime. I Want the Victory!*

53 *No More Victim. I Want the Victory!*

55 *No More Victime. I Want the Victory!*

57 No More Victime. I Want the Victory!

Then they cried to the LORD in their trouble, and He saved them from their distress. He sent out His Word and healed them; He rescued them from the grave. Let them give thanks to the Lord for His unfailing love and His wonderful deeds for mankind. ~ Psalm 107: 19-21

Love yourself, don't worry about your mother not being there for you. Be better than her, finish school, and don't try to live up to everyone else's expectations. Don't give up on your goals, you don't need anyone to validate you. You are your biggest fan, while it is okay to love others, love yourself first. Realize that what doesn't kill you, will make you stronger. You are destined for greatness and you have to believe it for yourself. Don't give up so easily when it seems difficult, finish what you started, you have so much potential. Stop hiding behind fear, value your self-worth, and don't let anyone take the very essence of you. ~SM

Prayer: Oh, sovereign God, you rescued me and you saved me. I now know what victory feels like. Thank you for your grace & mercy!

59 *No More Victime. I Want the Victory!*

61 *No More Victime. I Want the Victory!*

63 No More Victime. I Want the Victory!

65 *No More Victime. I Want the Victory!*

67 *No More Victime. I Want the Victory!*

69 *No More Victime. I Want the Victory!*

LORD my God, I called to you for help, and you healed me. ~ Psalm 30:2

First off, every person you thought or think will love you...you will be okay without them, I promise (lol). Stay in school and please don't leave it. I know you get bored easily but it will be worth it. Keep loving yourself, never lose that about yourself. Friends will come along that you just swear are your best friends but please know that in the end its only you. Be selfish about yourself when it comes to your happiness. Make sure you go to school to be a doctor because you will love it. If you do drugs and alcohol, it will be fun at first but in the end, it will destroy your life. If you are sad, talk to someone; lonely, talk to God. You are so amazing and you don't even know it. ~KR

Prayer: Lord, you are absolutely amazing! I can talk you, I can walk with you, and I can feel you in my Spirit. When all else fails, you are still there. Thank you for being my father and my Lord.

73 *No More Victim. I Want the Victory!*

75 *No More Victime. I Want the Victory!*

77 *No More Victime. I Want the Victory!*

79 *No More Victime. I Want the Victory!*

81 *No More Victime. I Want the Victory!*

83 *No More Victime. I Want the Victory!*

The LORD protects and preserves them-they are counted among the blessed in the land-He does not give them over to the desires of their foes. The LORD sustains them on their sickbed and restores them from their bed of illness. ~ Psalm 41:2-3

First off, your mother is always right. She just wants the best for you, so listen. Take heed to her advice. Be okay being you. Never take family or anyone for granted because you won't always have them to turn to. Life happens so don't rush. School is important and good grades so take it seriously. Believe you are enough, gain independence, don't depend on others, or let them decide how you feel. Don't give them that control. Go and visit your family more, they will do the best they know how to do. ~MK

Prayer: Lord, I pray for my family and my friends. I pray that as you heal me you restore to me the broken relationships that occurred over time. I pray for understanding and peace in the circumstances so that I can completely heal from my past hurt and pain.

85 *No More Victime. I Want the Victory!*

87 *No More Victime. I Want the Victory!*

89 *No More Victime. I Want the Victory!*

90   *Faith Ride to Victory!*

91 *No More Victime. I Want the Victory!*

93 *No More Victime. I Want the Victory!*

95 *No More Victime. I Want the Victory!*

97 *No More Victime. I Want the Victory!*

He heals the broken hearted and binds up their wounds
~ Psalm 147:3

Everything is going to be okay. I know you really like Anthony but he's not the one for you. He is going to introduce you to drugs and then he's going to break your heart. Drugs are going to lead you down a path you don't want to go on. You are going to have a baby, your baby will be taken away from you, your father will die. Save yourself from the heartache by doing what is right. Life is so much more important. You can overcome this and push through this by getting some help. Take time for yourself and for you to heal. Healing is possible. ~SS

Prayer: Lord, thank you for my children and my children's children. The greatest gift is the gift of LIFE. Thank you for your love and for healing this broken heart. Forgive me for where I fall short of your Glory.

99 *No More Victime. I Want the Victory!*

101 *No More Victime. I Want the Victory!*

103 *No More Victime. I Want the Victory!*

105 *No More Victime. I Want the Victory!*

107 *No More Victime. I Want the Victory!*

109 *No More Victime. I Want the Victory!*

He said to her, "Daughter, your faith has healed you. Go in peace and be freed you're your suffering." ~ Mark 5:34

If I could tell myself anything I would tell myself not to focus so much on the pain. Don't be afraid of being alone. Really, you aren't alone. God is with you. Enjoy all the time you have with your brothers because you are going to grow up really fast. Don't worry about being friends will all of these kids at school. They won't accept you for who you are. In the future, you will see that they never mattered anyway. Be all you can be, every time you get a chance to do something and be something. Wait until you meet your son, he is the ray of light in your world. Take care of him, be there for him, he loves you more than anything. ~BP

Prayer: Lord, I am afraid, I am broken, and I need a healing. I know you can take care of my fear and help me to increase my faith. My faith is what is going to help me get to victory.

113 *No More Victim. I Want the Victory!*

115 *No More Victime. I Want the Victory!*

117 *No More Victime. I Want the Victory!*

119 *No More Victime. I Want the Victory!*

121 *No More Victime. I Want the Victory!*

123 *No More Victime. I Want the Victory!*

Therefore, confess your sins to each other and pray for each other so that you may be healed. The prayer of a righteous person is powerful and effective. ~ *James 5:16*

Dear (person reading this)

I can tell you a lot about what to do or what not to do. We are not going to go there because everything that has happened and all of the choices you made has brought you to where you are today. Changing one choice could cost you what you live for today. Never give up. Be strong. Be you. Every day is an adventure. Keep the same enthusiasm and general happiness alive. Teach your little man to have the same qualities that everyone loves about you.

PS: Your mom and dad do love you, give them a break. ~RD

Prayer: Lord, I just want to be happy. Help me to be happy. Thank you for joy in my heart and peace in my Spirit. Thank you for change and thank you for restoration. In Jesus name, Amen.

125 *No More Victime. I Want the Victory!*

127 *No More Victime. I Want the Victory!*

129 *No More Victime. I Want the Victory!*

131 *No More Victime. I Want the Victory!*

133 *No More Victime. I Want the Victory!*

135 *No More Victime. I Want the Victory!*

For the LORD your God is the one who goes with you to fight for you against your enemies to give you victory. ~ Deuteronomy 20:4

I want to tell you that you are such a strong person. The way you are and the way you carry yourself. You are such a beautiful and inspiring woman. You never give up on what makes you happy. No matter how challenging the bumps in the road get, you still keep your head up for something better. You have been through a lot, some good, some bad. You have learned and experienced. Remember, God is not going to give you anything you can't handle. You are a sucker for love, driven by passion. You always believe in yourself and your dreams. Ask for help, respect yourself, and your parents. Read the bible, you will be surprised at how it will change your life. I love you. ~JP

Prayer: Thank you Lord for fighting for me and on my behalf. There were times where I didn't think I was going to make it but you Lord, have pulled me through.

139 *No More Victime. I Want the Victory!*

141 *No More Victime. I Want the Victory!*

143 *No More Victime. I Want the Victory!*

145 *No More Victime. I Want the Victory!*

147 *No More Victime. I Want the Victory!*

149 *No More Victime. I Want the Victory!*

I have told you these things, so that in me you may have peace. In this world you will have trouble. But take heart! I have overcome the world! ~ John 16:33

From the LORD comes deliverance. May your blessing be on your people. ~ Psalm 3:8

For everyone born of God overcomes the world. This is the victory that has overcome the world, even our faith. ~ I John 5:4

What, then, shall we say in response to these things? If God is for us, who can be against us? ~ Romans 8:31

But thanks be to God! He gives us the victory through our Lord Jesus Christ. ~ I Corinthians 15:57

I want for each and every one of you to know, no matter what comes your way, keep fighting for your recovery, for your children, for your self-worth, for your success, and keep fighting for your LIFE! No matter how tired, no matter how frustrated, no matter how upset something or someone gets, keep FIGHTING! When you feel like giving up, push yourself harder to keep going. It is not easy, but it is easier than being in jail or on the streets, or from house to house living in misery. You have all suffered enough, why suffer anymore? Take this opportunity to be what you never thought you could be. Become that person you have always wanted to be. Just sit still, listen, use the tools you learned, find your higher power, work on yourself and you will succeed. Give yourself what no one else ever gave, let go of all of the hurt & pain, grab hold of all of the love & happiness.

Let go of all of the negative people that is still hurting you, why talk to them? They will keep you from what you need. Don't cheat yourself and don't cheat your children. Break this cycle of hurt and pain, give yourself and your children a life that you have dreamed of having. You have survived all of the bad, so you can survive this road to happiness. You lose when you quit and when you give up, don't give up. Make the changes you need to make, do in your heart what you know you need to do. You are going to make mistakes and deal with things you have never dealt with before but learn from your mistakes and deal with those things. Once you realize that you can, you will feel so good about yourself. You will want to do better and you have to want it in order to get it. So, want more than you have ever wanted and go get it with all you have in you. And remember that God is with you every step of the way. Believe and never stop believing you can succeed and you can be and have whatever your heart desires.

Love, DC

Ending prayer:

Dear Lord, thank you for giving me hope, faith, and truth. Thank you for true victory in you. Thank you for allowing me to take this ride and journey in my life. For, I didn't know that in my past life was going to be difficult but I now know that since I have you, life will be much simpler. I no longer have to walk in shame or guilt. I can feel the same freedom that you shared with us when your son Jesus Christ died on the cross for our sins. Thank you for abundance and for the power of victory. Thank you for love, patience, kindness, gentleness, and self-control. Thank you for teaching me your ways and helping me to correct my errors. I ask that you continue to be with me and continue to lead and guide me. I ask that you care for my family and care for my friends. For I want everyone in my life that is important to me to feel your Spirit of victory. For now I am truly confident that you care for me and you love me. I now believe that all things forward in my life will work out for my good. In Christ name, Amen.

Made in the USA
Columbia, SC
01 January 2023